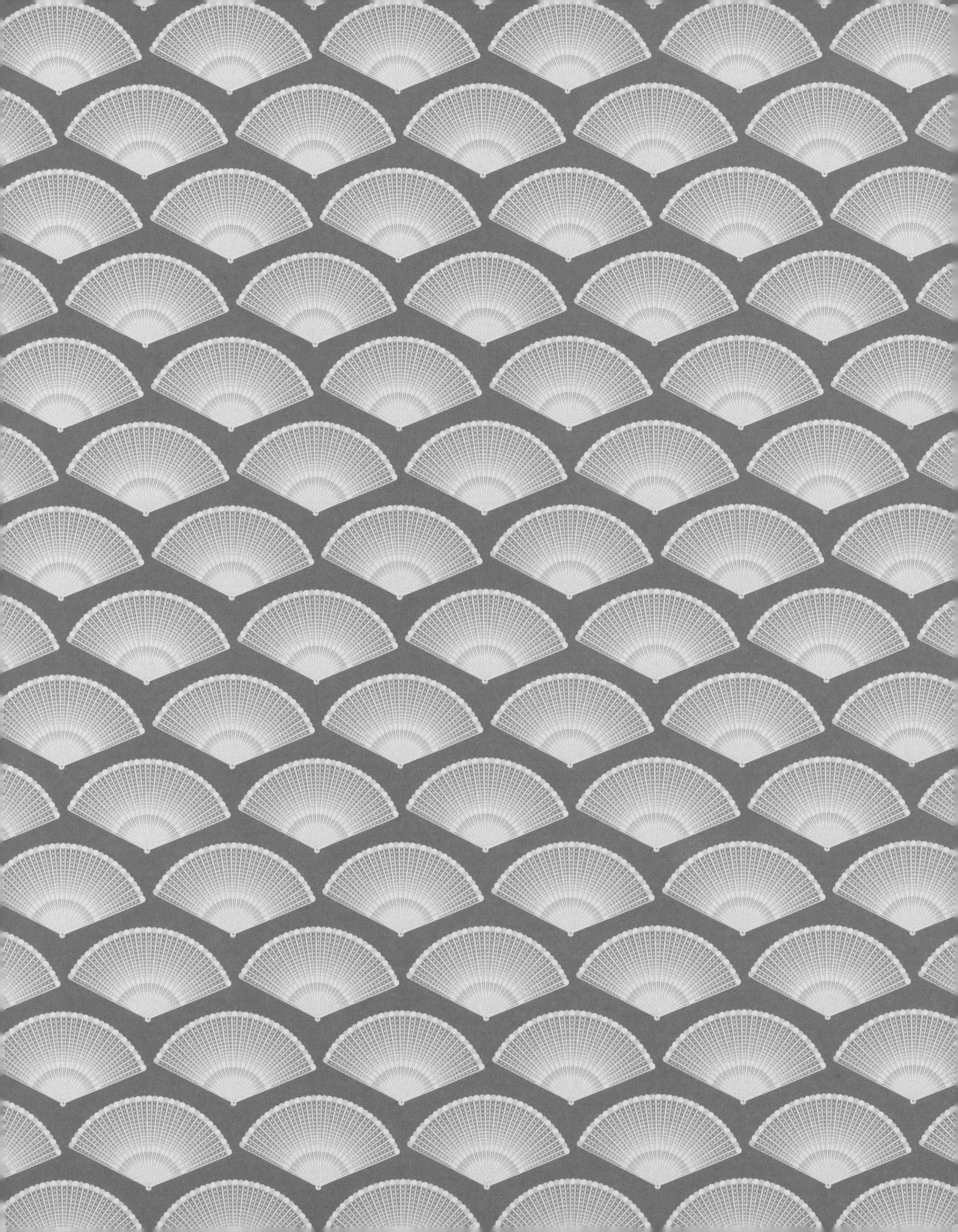

JANE AUSTEN

GREAT LIVES IN GRAPHICS

Button
BOOKS

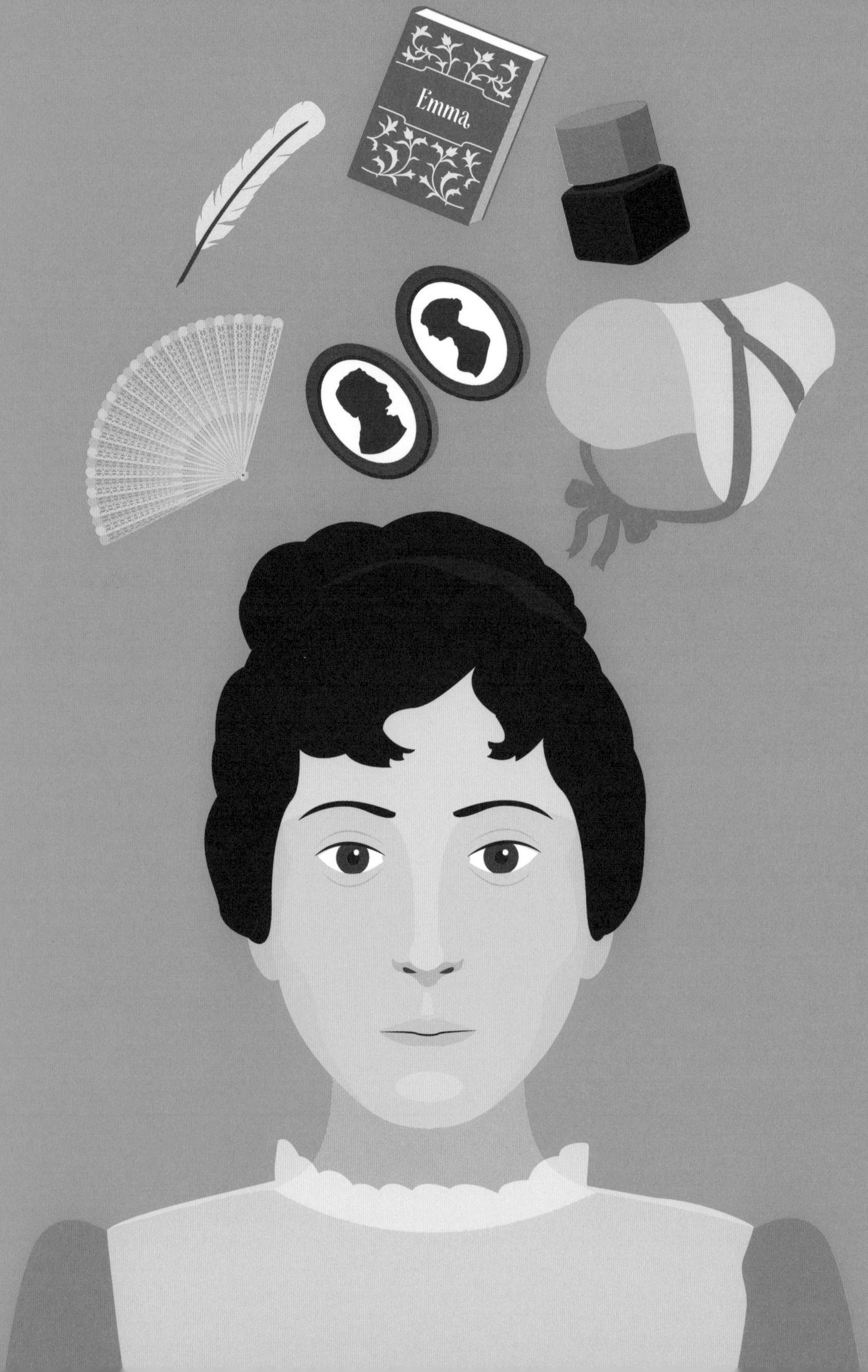
Emma

Jane Austen is one of the most famous writers in the world. She completed only six major novels, but those stories have captivated audiences for more than 200 years. Some readers love them for their real-life characters, others for their romantic plot lines, or dashing heroes. But the reason she has been compared to the likes of Shakespeare is her special talent for portraying people as they truly are. Writing at a time when appearances were everything, Jane was a master at revealing what people were really thinking behind their polite smiles.

Sadly, because Regency women weren't encouraged to read, let alone write, Jane hid her identity and people only found out she was the author of her books after she died. If she was alive today imagine her surprise to find she's now so popular there's even a name for her thousands of fans: Janeites. Read on to discover if you might become one of them...

Jane's WORLD

1791 Titanium discovered

22
Ti
Titanium

1789 French Revolution begins

1793 Britain goes to war with France

1775
Jane Austen is born on December 16 in Steventon, Hampshire, UK

1788
King George III has breakdown

1795 Jane meets Tom Lefroy

J.A. T.L.

1779
Captain Cook dies

R.I.P.

1800
Italian Alessandro Volta makes the first battery

1783 Jane and Cassandra sent away to school

1787
Begins to write stories and poems, later called juvenilia

1801
Austen family moves to Bath. Great Britain and Ireland united as UK

1802

Harris Bigg-Wither proposes to Jane. Jane says yes, then no

1812

Charles Dickens is born

1813

Pride and Prejudice published

1814

Mansfield Park published

1804

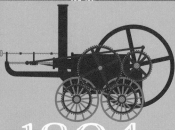

World's first steam-powered railway journey occurs in Wales

1811

Sense and Sensibility published. George, Prince of Wales, is Prince Regent

1815

Emma published. Napoleon defeated at Battle of Waterloo

1805

Jane's dad dies. Battle of Trafalgar

1816

Jane falls ill

1817

Jane dies on July 18 in Winchester; *Northanger Abbey* and *Persuasion* published

1806

Austen family leaves Bath

1807

UK outlaws the slave trade

R.I.P.

JULY 18 1817 (Age 41)

STORY *corner*

Jane was born in a village in the English countryside called Steventon where her dad, George Austen, was the rector. The seventh of eight children, Jane had a large family and they all lived together in the rambling old rectory.

AT 3 MONTHS OLD

Jane was packed off to stay with a wet nurse in the village, where she lived for at least a year before returning home as a toddler. This was normal for babies born into the gentry in the 18th century!

 1x 👩 6x

Along with her six brothers and older sister Cassandra, Jane spent most of her time reading aloud, dancing, playing card games, doing puzzles, and putting on plays.

 When her sister Cassandra was sent away to school, Jane missed her so much she was allowed to join her, aged just seven. Her mom said: "If Cassandra's head had been going to be cut off, Jane would have hers cut off too."

 Jane's **MOM** was known for her quick wit and often wrote funny rhyming notes to the children.

Jane's dad owned lots of books and encouraged his children to read authors like Shakespeare and Samuel Johnson.

500+ BOOKS

The rectory had
10 BEDROOMS
3 IN THE ATTIC

To make some extra cash Jane's dad set up a mini-boarding school and tutored boys who came to live with them. £££££

Jane **LIKED TO PLAY**

BILBOCATCH
(a cup and ball game)

AGE 12

The family was respectable but not rich. They had a cook and a maid living with them–maids usually started work young, around 12!

The Austen family had several farm animals, grew vegetables, and made mead.

BULL **COWS**

DUCKS **TURKEYS** **CHICKENS**

JANE WAS 11

when she started writing silly stories, plays, and poetry. Called her "juvenilia" by scholars, one early tale tells the story of three sisters fighting not to be the one to marry the village's only (ugly) single man.

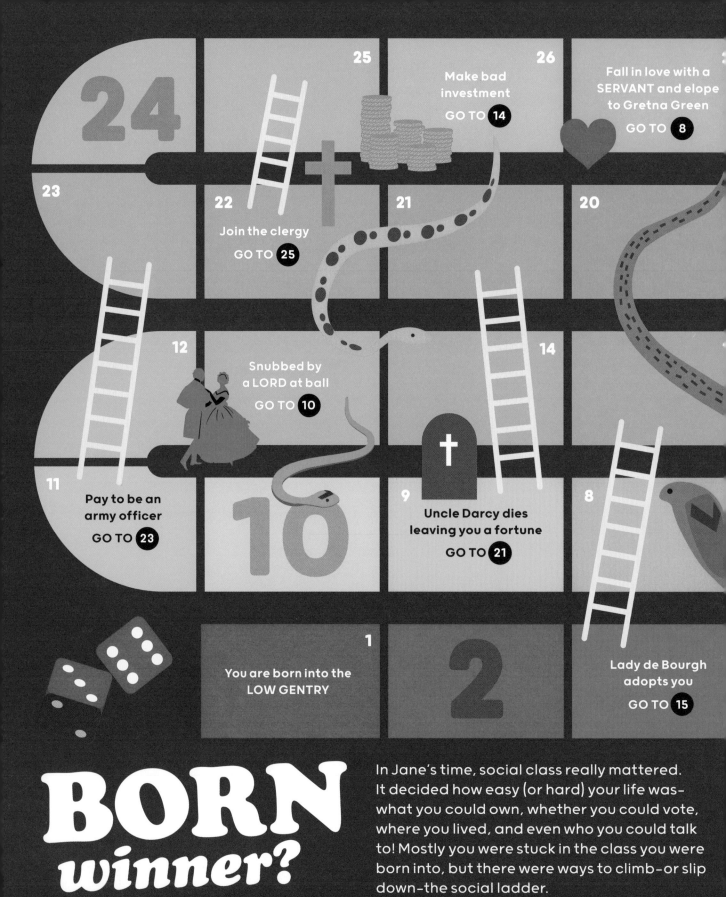

25

26
Make bad investment
GO TO **14**

Fall in love with a SERVANT and elope to Gretna Green
GO TO **8**

24

23

22
Join the clergy
GO TO **25**

21

20

12
Snubbed by a LORD at ball
GO TO **10**

14

11
Pay to be an army officer
GO TO **23**

10

9
Uncle Darcy dies leaving you a fortune
GO TO **21**

8

1
You are born into the LOW GENTRY

2

Lady de Bourgh adopts you
GO TO **15**

BORN
winner?

In Jane's time, social class really mattered. It decided how easy (or hard) your life was—what you could own, whether you could vote, where you lived, and even who you could talk to! Mostly you were stuck in the class you were born into, but there were ways to climb–or slip down–the social ladder.

28

FINISH!

Well done! You've moved up into the NOBILITY.

9

18

16

17

Gamble at cards,
lose inheritance

GO TO 6

7

6

4

You marry a
LORD / LADY

GO TO 28

5

DID YOU KNOW?

Only around 1.5% of the population was landed gentry, but they had most of the wealth and power.

MONEY TALKS!

Annual salary during the Regency period

£800+	Landed gentry
£700	Very comfortable
£250	Low gentry
£150	Tradesmen
£50	Edge of poverty

PECKING ORDER

Here's who was where on the social ladder in Jane's time...

ROYALTY
Kings, queens, princes, princesses

NOBILITY
Lords, earls, dukes

LANDED GENTRY
Baronets, knights, landowners

JANE AUSTEN'S SOCIAL POSITION

LOW GENTRY
Clergy, lawyers, bankers, doctors, wealthy merchants, MPs, army/navy officers

TRADESMEN & ARTISANS
Teachers, shopkeepers, butchers, bakers, shoemakers

SERVANTS
Butlers, housekeepers

LABORERS
Farm laborers, maids, stable hands, gardeners, factory workers

POOR
Paupers, vagrants, gypsies, criminals

1 STEVENTON, HAMPSHIRE

Jane lived at the old rectory until she was 25.

2 ROWLING, KENT

Jane visited her brother Edward and his 11 children (wow!) for dinner and dancing at Goodnestone House.

3 BASINGSTOKE, HAMPSHIRE

Jane attended her first balls here with her sister.

4 GODMERSHAM PARK, KENT

Lucky Edward was adopted by wealthy relatives and became sole heir to their palatial estates. Jane visited him often.

Because journeys could take several days, coaching inns were a common sight on English roads. They offered cheap rooms and travelers would often share a bed with two or three strangers!

CLEVER CLOGS

Ladies wore metal "pattens" over their slippers to keep their feet out of the mud.

SYDNEY PLACE

SOMERSET

9

LONDON

7

HAMPSHIRE

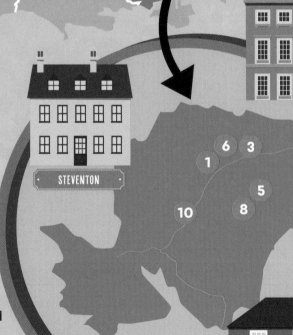

STEVENTON

6 3
1
5
8
10

CHAWTON

ROCKY ROAD

Like many of the gentry in the Regency era, Jane had a busy schedule visiting friends and relatives all over England, touring grand houses, and mixing with the super-rich at fancy balls and private parties. But getting from place to place wasn't always easy...

5 ALTON, HAMPSHIRE

Jane and Cassandra strolled to the shops in Alton from Chawton.

6 MANYDOWN PARK, HAMPSHIRE

While Jane and Cassandra were visiting friends Catherine and Althea Bigg, their brother Harris proposed to Jane. She said yes, but changed her mind the next day!

7 BATH, SOMERSET

When Jane's dad retired the family moved to Bath–much to her dismay.

8 CHAWTON, HAMPSHIRE

After Jane's dad died, the Austens settled in a cottage on her brother Edward's estate. Today the house is a museum.

GOODNESTONE HOUSE

9 HANS PLACE, LONDON

When Jane traveled to London to meet with publishers she stayed with her brother Henry at his flat in Knightsbridge.

10 WINCHESTER, HAMPSHIRE

Jane fell ill and died in her sister's arms at a hospital in Winchester, aged just 41.

KENT

SPEED OF TRAVEL

ON FOOT 3MPH
Jane probably walked 2 or 3 miles a day.

BAROUCHE 4MPH
Heavy carriage on London's paved roads.

CHAISE 6MPH
One-horse carriage on country lanes.

MAIL COACH 8MPH
Traveled day and night, whatever the weather!

CURRICLE 13MPH
Sports chariot at full pelt.

WHY WAS TRAVEL SO TRICKY IN REGENCY ENGLAND?

- Country roads were muddy and potholed.
- Long and uncomfortable journeys.
- Most people traveled on foot.
- Inappropriate for women to travel alone.
- No travel on Sundays.
- Highwaymen made traveling dangerous.
- No electric lights meant daytime travel only, or by moonlight.

REGENCY RULES

1. People in the Regency era only hung out with others of the same class.
2. All gentry living in the same neighborhood were expected to mix socially, whether they liked each other or not!

BOOKS

Jane began writing as a teenager, but her first novel wasn't published until she was 35. At the time there was a craze for gothic stories featuring spooky castles, supernatural beings, and hysterical women. Jane ignored all that. She was interested in real life and the challenges facing women of her class, whose best chance at happiness was finding a rich husband.

Two sisters looking for marriage and love have to decide if they follow head or heart.

Witty young woman and arrogant gentleman realize first impressions aren't always right.

Timid goody two-shoes overcomes social challenges to win the day.

Sense & Sensibility

SISTER ACT

WORLD FAMOUS ROM-COM

Pride & Prejudice

MANSFIELD PARK

MORALS AND MISUNDER-STANDING

PUBLISHED
1811

HEROINES
Elinor & Marianne Dashwood

LOVE INTERESTS
Edward Ferrars & Colonel Brandon

QUIET ACTIVISM
Questions a system that leaves women with little power or wealth.

PUBLISHED
1813

HEROINE
Elizabeth Bennet

LOVE INTEREST
Fitzwilliam Darcy

QUIET ACTIVISM
Examines Regency traditions and women's place in society.

PUBLISHED
1814

HEROINE
Fanny Price

LOVE INTEREST
Edmund Bertram

QUIET ACTIVISM
Questions the slave trade and the upper classes for choosing to ignore its evils.

Misguided heroine meddles in friends' affairs before facing up to her flaws.

Girl jilts love of her life because he's low class, rekindles romance when he climbs social ladder.

Naïve young girl's love of gothic romance novels leads her to make some not-great life choices.

Emma,

PERSUASION

MILITARY MOVES

NORTHANGER ABBEY

MATCHMAKING MADNESS

COMING OF AGE COMEDY

PUBLISHED
1815

HEROINE
Emma Woodhouse

LOVE INTEREST
Mr. Knightley

QUIET ACTIVISM
Condemns a society that doesn't care for the poor and vulnerable.

PUBLISHED
1817

HEROINE
Anne Elliot

LOVE INTEREST
Captain Wentworth

QUIET ACTIVISM
Asks whether people should inherit social power or have to work for it.

PUBLISHED
1817

HEROINE
Catherine Morland

LOVE INTEREST
Henry Tilney

QUIET ACTIVISM
Urges women to live in the real world.

People thought women writing for money was pretty shocking during the Regency! To keep her reputation intact, Jane published her books anonymously under the pseudonym:

A. Lady

SMASH THE PATRIARCHY

Regency

In Jane's time people in England had some funny ideas about what girls born into the gentry could and couldn't do. Women's rights in the West have come a long way since then, but there's still work to do…

GIRLS EDUCATED UNTIL AGE: 12

SUBJECTS STUDIED: Needlework, dancing, drawing, English, math, and French.

Not allowed to vote.

Not expected to work.

Not allowed to go to university.

BEST CHANCE OF HAPPINESS: Marriage.

ADMIRABLE QUALITIES:

Quiet

Delicate

Modest

RIGHTS AS A WIFE? Husband owns everything.

RIGHTS TO OWN CHILDREN? Husband decides.

And obviously a woman couldn't enter politics!

MARY ROCKS!

Writer Mary Wollstonecraft–aka the "Mother of Feminism"–argued for improved education for women during Jane's time.

NOW!

WOMEN FINALLY GET VOTE! ✕

In 1918, the UK government passed an Act giving women over the age of 30 who were householders or married to a householder the vote. It was only in 1928 that women were granted exactly the same voting rights as men.

Right to vote.

Right to choose career.

Very few women in top leadership roles

Right to equal education.

Right to own property.

ADMIRABLE QUALITIES:

Be yourself!

 Women still not paid as much as men for same jobs.

FUTURE?

$ Equal pay for men and women.

More women in leadership roles.

Less violence against women.

DID YOU KNOW?

During her lifetime the average woman will do seven years more unpaid work (childcare, cleaning, cooking etc) than a man!

Strictly BALLROOM

Jane loved dancing and balls were a great way for girls to find a husband. They were one of the few times young men and women could hang out and flirt without a chaperone standing right over them. Plus there was always plenty of gossip–who danced with who, who ignored someone else, who seemed especially close. But this was still the Regency, and that meant strict rules...

RULE №2

Men must wear short breeches and stockings.

RULE №1

Fashionable balls open with a Minuet dance.

RULE №4

No dancing with anyone until you've been formally introduced.

RULE №3

No turning your nose up at the fancy finger foods–chicken stuffed with pig's tongue is a delicacy!

YUCK!

Jane included a ball scene in every one of her novels. They gave her the perfect opportunity to reveal her characters' true personalities according to what they said and how they behaved, plus develop any romances.

RULE №5

Refuse to dance with someone and you can't dance with anyone else.

RULE №7

No leaving the floor until the dance is finished.

RULE №8

Dances are 15 minutes to half an hour long—ouch!

RULE №6

No hissing, clapping, snapping your fingers, or howling.

RULE №10

Never dance more than twice with the same person.

RULE №9

When you're not dancing, hang out at the edge and gossip about everyone else.

PSSSTTT...

BLAH, BLAH

DID YOU KNOW?

When Jane was 20 she met law student **TOM LEFROY**, who was visiting his aunt and uncle near Steventon. After flirting together at several balls some historians think Jane fell in love with him, but his family wasn't happy with the match and Tom married someone else, leaving Jane heartbroken.

COLORFUL CHARACTERS

Not long after she turned 20, Jane began writing her most famous novel–*Pride and Prejudice*. Filled with some of her best characters, from slimy Mr. Collins to catty Caroline Bingley, it follows the sparkling Lizzie Bennet as she and her romantic hero Mr. Darcy learn that first impressions aren't always right. Who would you be?

Elizabeth Bennet
HEROINE

SKILLS: Clever, sensible
WIT: ■■■■■■■■■
ATTRACTION: ■■■■■■■■
WEALTH: ◉◉◉◉◯◯◯◯◯◯◯
KINDNESS: ■■■■■■■■
WEAKNESS: Prejudiced

Mr. Darcy
HERO

SKILLS: Smart, honest
WIT: ■■■■■■■■
ATTRACTION: ■■■■■■■■■
WEALTH: ◉◉◉◉◉◉◉◉◉◉◉
KINDNESS: ■■■■■■■
WEAKNESS: Proud

Charles Bingley
DARCY'S BEST FRIEND

SKILLS: Easygoing, generous
WIT: ■■■■■
ATTRACTION: ■■■■■■
WEALTH: ◉◉◉◉◉◉◉◉◉
KINDNESS: ■■■■■■■■■
WEAKNESS: Indecisive

Jane Bennet
ELIZABETH'S OLDER SISTER

SKILLS: Gentle, innocent
WIT: ■■■■■■
ATTRACTION: ■■■■■■■■
WEALTH: ◉◉◉◉◯◯◯◯◯◯◯
KINDNESS: ■■■■■■■■
WEAKNESS: Naive

"At length the day is come on which I am to flirt my last with Tom Lefroy... My tears flow as I write, at the melancholy idea."

Letter from Jane to her sister Cassandra, 1796

George Wickham

VILLAIN

SKILLS: Charming, soldier

WIT: ■■■■■■■■□□

ATTRACTION: ■■■■■■■□□□

WEALTH: ◉◉◉◉◉◉◉◉◉◉

KINDNESS: ■■■□□□□□□□

WEAKNESS: Greedy

Caroline Bingley

CHARLES'S SISTER

SKILLS: Elegant, well-connected

WIT: ■■■■■■■□□□

ATTRACTION: ■■■■■■■□□□

WEALTH: ◉◉◉◉◉◉◉◉◉◉

KINDNESS: ■■■■■■□□□□

WEAKNESS: Snobbish

Mr. Collins

FOOL

SKILLS: Clergyman, traditional

WIT: ■■■□□□□□□□

ATTRACTION: ■□□□□□□□□□

WEALTH: ◉◉◉◉◉◉◉◉◉◉

KINDNESS: ■■■■■□□□□□

WEAKNESS: Pompous

Lydia Bennet

ELIZABETH'S YOUNGER SISTER

SKILLS: Energetic, fun

WIT: ■■■■■■■■■□

ATTRACTION: ■■■■■■□□□□

WEALTH: ◉◉◉◉◉◉◉◉◉◉

KINDNESS: ■■■■■■■□□□

WEAKNESS: Selfish

Jane sold the copyright for *Pride and Prejudice* to her publishers for

£110

The book was an instant hit–in the past 200 years it's sold **20 MILLION COPIES** and has never been out of print!

GAME OVER

Lady of LETTERS

Jane spent a huge amount of her time writing–when she wasn't penning books, she was composing letters, mostly to her beloved sister.

George

Age 29

Jane's dad dies and she moves several times with Cassandra and her mom.

Age 25

Jane's dad retires and the family move to Bath. Jane doesn't like it and stops writing.

Age 15

At 15 Jane wrote *The History of England*, a 34-page booklet that makes fun of English kings and queens, including silly drawings by her sister Cassandra.

Metal pen nibs existed at the time Jane was writing, but they were expensive, so she used a quill. Quills were usually made from goose feathers...

1 Take a goose feather.

2 Heat feather to harden.

3 Carefully cut to make a nib.

Age 18

Jane begins writing Lady Susan, about a horrid, flirty woman. Cassandra gets engaged to one of her dad's former pupils, Thomas Fowle.

Age 22

Jane finishes her first version of Sense and Sensibility.

Sense & Sensibility

Age 21

Cassandra's fiancé Thomas Fowle dies of yellow fever on an expedition to the West Indies. Before he leaves, she vows to remain faithful and never marry anyone else.

YELLOW FEVER

Age 19

Jane starts Elinor and Marianne, later to be called *Sense and Sensibility*. She meets law student Tom Lefroy.

J.A. T.L.

Age 20

Jane sees Tom Lefroy for the last time. Begins writing First Impressions, later called *Pride and Prejudice*.

Age 33

Jane's brother Edward offers them the use of a cottage on his estate. Jane starts writing again.

Edward

Age 35

Jane begins *Mansfield Park*. *Sense and Sensibility* is published to good reviews.

Pride & Prejudice

Age 37

Pride and Prejudice is published.

BEST SELLER

Age 38

Mansfield Park is published in May and sells out by October.

Age 39

Jane finishes writing *Emma* and starts *The Elliots* (later called *Persuasion*).

Age 40

Jane becomes ill, but continues to write *Persuasion*.

SISTER ACT

Jane shared a room with her sister Cassandra for her whole life. Whenever they were apart— occasionally they visited friends separately— they wrote to each other almost every day. After Jane died Cassandra destroyed hundreds of her letters, probably to protect her privacy.

Cassandra

OUT OF AN ESTIMATED **3,000 LETTERS** ONLY AROUND **160** SURVIVE TODAY

Cassandra lived alone until she died, aged 72. Over the next 100 years Jane's notebooks were nearly forgotten. They made their way down the family tree until they ended up in the hands of her brother Francis's granddaughter's niece, who sold them to the British Library at auction in July 1977.

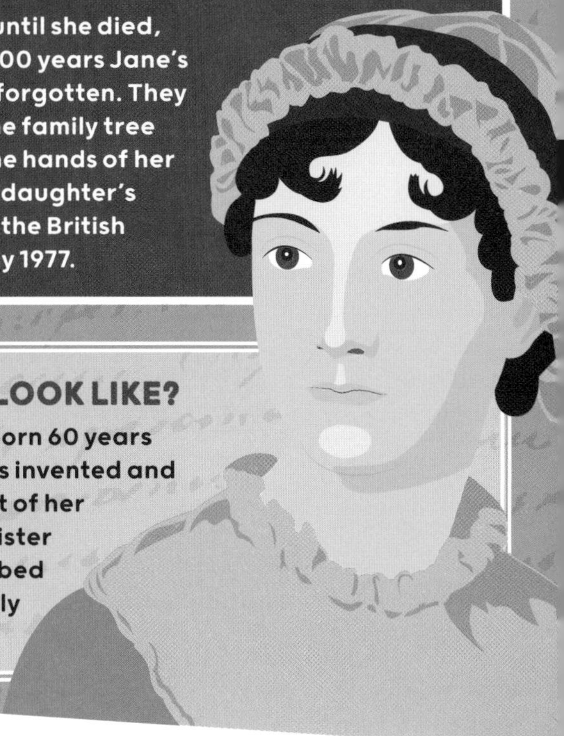

WHAT DID JANE LOOK LIKE?

No one knows. She was born 60 years before photography was invented and the only verified portrait of her is a small sketch by her sister Cassandra, later described by her niece as "hideously unlike" her!

Age 41

Jane dies and is buried in Winchester Cathedral. Cassandra writes:

"I have lost a treasure, such a sister, such a friend as never can have been surpassed. She was the sun of my life, the gilder of every pleasure, the soother of every sorrow, I had not a thought concealed from her, and it is as if I had lost a part of myself."

Northanger Abbey and Persuasion are published after Jane's death, in her own name for the first time.

Georgie Porgie!

When Jane was young, King George III was on the throne. By the time her first novel was published, he was suffering from poor mental health and his son George, the Prince Regent, took over from 1811 to 1820–hence the "Regency" era. Unfortunately, the Prince had an enormous appetite. He ate too much, drank too much, gambled too much, and spent too much until, finally, his body could take no more...

Food glorious food

The Prince hosted incredible banquets, sometimes serving over 100 dishes, including such exotic recipes as jellied partridge and tart of thrushes!

Champagne

Roast pig's head

CELERY SOUP

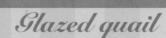

Glazed quail   **Pigeons in crayfish butter**

Plain Jane

A fan of Jane's fiction, the Prince asked her to dedicate a book to him and she was invited to tour his home in London. Jane was unimpressed by his extravagances but the request of a prince wasn't something to be taken lightly so she (unenthusiastically) dedicated Emma to him when it was published.

Larger than life!

He had a fantastic vacation home built–the Royal Pavilion in Brighton–but eventually grew too big to climb upstairs and had to sleep on the ground floor!

England's top 10,000 aristocrats were known as **The Ton**, from the French phrase "le bon ton," meaning "good manners".

The Prince spent a whopping

£240,000
(around $8 million today)

on his coronation–20 times the amount his dad spent when he was crowned!

Took **3 hours** to lace him into his corset.

Cataracts left him almost blind.

Had an enlarged heart.

55-inch waist.

Doctors found an orange-sized tumor in his bladder.

Gout in his hands and feet meant he couldn't write.

Legs filled with fluid.

Zzz

Unable to lie down in case the weight of his chest suffocated him.

Died after popping a blood vessel in his stomach while on the toilet!

WEIGHT

336 LB
(152 kg)

Jane's books have been made into movies countless times, but few are as good as 90s teen classic *Clueless*. Based on *Emma*, both stories follow slightly spoiled heroines as they try to fix up friends with the perfect date.

Emma

FASHION VICTIM SCALE

EMMA WOODHOUSE

AGE:
21

SOCIAL STATUS:
Gentry

STOMPING GROUND:
English village

NEW BFF:
Harriet Smith

FAVORITE PASTIMES:
Makeovers & matchmaking

RICH?
Y£S!

No. of years since character created:
200+

"I always deserve the best treatment, because I never put up with any other"

CRUSH: **Frank Churchill**

BAE: **Mr. Knightley**

Cher

FASHION VICTIM SCALE

"As if!"

CHER HOROWITZ

SOCIAL STATUS: Popular

AGE: 15

STOMPING GROUND: Beverly Hills high school

NEW BFF: Tai Frasier

FAVORITE PASTIMES: Makeovers & matchmaking

RICH? V£RY!

CRUSH: Christian Stovitz

BAE: Josh Lucas

No. of years since character created: 25+

WORLD AT WAR

For almost all of Jane's life, Britain was at war–with France from 1793 to 1815 (apart from a couple of short breaks) and with America for three years from 1812. Two of her brothers were in the navy and one joined the militia. Jane wrote books based on real life in the present day, yet the war is hardly mentioned. Why? Probably because Jane had to be careful about what she said. She was a woman writing at a dangerous time in history.

320,000
PRUSSIANS

750,000
BRITISH

900,000
RUSSIANS

1,000,000
AUSTRIANS

3,000,000
FRENCH

NAPOLEONIC IN NUMBERS

While Jane was writing her novels, France's greatest general, Napoleon Bonaparte, was storming across Europe, battling against Britain, Prussia, Austria, and Russia.

Sugar rush

Sugar became so popular among the upper classes in Regency times it led to an **EPIDEMIC OF TOOTH DECAY**. The British **PULLED TEETH** from the bodies of **DEAD SOLDIERS** to make dentures and those that came from the young, fit men who died at the Battle of Waterloo in 1815 (called Waterloo Teeth) were especially popular.

URGGGHHHH!

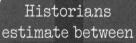
Historians estimate between **3-5 MILLION** people died in the Napoleonic Wars between 1803 and 1815.

ALL AT SEA

How navies around the world compared in 1792.

KEY

○ Great Britain
○ France
○ Spain
○ Russia
○ Holland

VESSELS

- 661
- 803
- 291
- 222
- 187

CANNON

- 14,000
- 12,000
- 10,000
- 9,000
- 2,300

CREW

- 100,000
- 78,000
- 50,000
- 21,000
- 15,000

BATTLE OF TRAFALGAR

British Royal Navy ships led by Admiral Nelson won against the French and Spanish fleets in 1805 for three main reasons:

1 TEAMWORK

Most British sailors had been working and living together on the same ship for at least two years.

2 TECHNOLOGY

British ships had better guns that could fire faster.

3 LEADERSHIP

Admiral Nelson died in the battle, but it was his masterful plan that led Britain to victory and established it as a global naval power for the next 100 years.

The REGENCY Name Generator

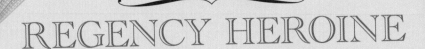

Can you find your Regency name–and the name of your hero or heroine–using this generator?

REGENCY HEROINE

Last number in your age	First name initial	Last name initial	Favorite color	Birthday
0 Lady	A Sophia	A Carter	RED Haughty	JANUARY Plays piano beautifully
1 Countess	B Anne	B Morris	GREEN Gentle	FEBRUARY Has read 500 books
2 Marchioness	C Elizabeth	C Harrington	BLUE Audacious	MARCH Enjoys painting portraits
3 Duchess	D Fanny	D Metcalfe	YELLOW Delicate	APRIL Loves a good gossip
4 Dame	E Cassandra	E Warwick	PINK Witty	MAY Is a clever conversationalist
5 Baroness	F Georgiana	F Townshend	ORANGE Stylish	JUNE Dances the Minuet gracefully
6 Miss	G Jane	G Windham	PURPLE Frivolous	JULY Can write an artful letter
7 Viscountess	H Louisa	H Russell	BROWN Modest	AUGUST Speaks both French and Italian
8 Mrs.	I Diana	I Pemberton	PEACH Passionate	SEPTEMBER Plans to elope to Gretna Green
9 Madam	J Kitty	J Nicholson	SILVER Kind	OCTOBER Likes to draw flowers and plants
	K Elinor	K Jennings	TURQUOISE Elegant	NOVEMBER Is an accomplished seamstress
	L Julia	L Harding	GOLD Cheerful	DECEMBER Sings like a nightingale
	M Esther	M Hill		
	N Eliza	N Campbell		
	O Margaret	O Browning		
	P Frances	P Blackmore		
	Q Catherine	Q Frampton		
	R Harriet	R Haddington		
	S Dorothea	S Hughes		
	T Isabella	T Mowbray		
	U Charlotte	U Ridlington		
	V Emma	V Croft		
	W Clara	W Walford		
	X Lydia	X Leeson		
	Y Susan	Y Honeyfield		
	Z Marianne	Z Godwin		

Viscountess Isabella Harding
Elegant and has read 500 books

REGENCY HERO

Last number in your age	First name initial	Last name initial	Favorite color	Birthday
0 Colonel	A George	A Darcy	RED Independent	JANUARY Fishes for salmon in the River Dove
1 Lord	B Nicholas	B Willoughby	GREEN Wise	FEBRUARY Goes riding after breakfast
2 Dr.	C Edward	C Elliot	BLUE Strong	MARCH Earns £10,000 a year
3 Captain	D William	D Thorpe	YELLOW Cultured	
4 Mr.	E Thomas	E Sidney	PINK Sporty	APRIL Owns a stately home
5 Sir	F James	F Fairfax	ORANGE Courteous	MAY Reads Greek and Latin
6 Earl	G Arthur	G Taylor	PURPLE Extravagant	JUNE Hangs out in Gentlemen's Clubs
7 Marquess	H Stephen	H Tilney	BROWN Honorable	JULY Gallops after foxes
8 Baron	I Edmund	I Knightley	PEACH Manly	AUGUST Manages the estate
9 Duke	J Alexander	J Palmer	SILVER Hen-pecked	SEPTEMBER Shows off fencing skills
	K Benjamin	K Philadelphia	BURGUNDY Awkward	OCTOBER Learns to box
	L Robert	L Barton	GOLD Honest	NOVEMBER Races a curricle carriage
	M Charles	M Weston		DECEMBER Sets off on Grand Tour of Europe
	N Peter	N Morland		
	O Richard	O Parker		
	P Horace	P Brandon		
	Q Joseph	Q Pemberley		
	R Samuel	R Woodhouse		
	S Isaac	S Bingley		
	T Frederick	T Perry		
	U Matthew	U Lucas		
	V Francis	V Croft		
	W Henry	W Russell		
	X Christopher	X Bennet		
	Y Oliver	Y Middleton		
	Z Philip	Z Dashwood		

Marquess Edmund Bingley
Extravagant and owns
a stately home

Fan club

It's over 200 years since her first novel was published, but around the world Jane's books have more readers than ever. In the US, fan worship is on a similar level to that of *Star Trek* and *Harry Potter*. The Jane Austen Society of North America (Jasna) has more than:

Calling themselves Janeites, some fans write their own romantic stories, while others dress up in Regency clothes and throw Jane Austen-themed tea parties and balls!

WE ♥ JANE!

5,000 members : 80 branches

JANEITES

According to Jasna, here's what the typical Janeite is like:

AGE **40**

NATIONALITY **English-speaking**

JOB **Teacher or librarian**

EDUCATION **College degree or higher**

HOBBIES **Reading, watching movies, listening to music**

FAVORITE DRINK **Tea**

PETS **Cat**

AGE DISCOVERED JANE **Before 17**

FAVORITE JANE BOOK *Pride and Prejudice*

FAVORITE BAD BOY **George Wickham**

FAVORITE COMIC CHARACTERS **Mrs. Bennet, Mr. Collins**

FAVORITE HEROINE **Elizabeth Bennet**

FAVORITE HERO **Mr. Darcy**

It wasn't that long ago that Janeites were mostly men–*Jungle Book* author Rudyard Kipling printed a short story called *Janeites* in 1924 about a group of World War I soldiers who loved Jane's books.

The Oxford English Dictionary says Jane was the first to use more than 40 words, including:

DINNER PARTY

SPONGECAKE

DOORBELL

For many years Jane was thought of as a cynical critic of society rather than a romantic novelist. What do you think?

Jane's books have been translated into more than

40 LANGUAGES

...and inspired more than

60

movie and TV adaptations.

WHICH BOOK SHOULD YOU READ FIRST?

Readers' choice

Critics' choice

THE WATSONS · 1871

Sense and Sensibility · 1811

PRIDE AND PREJUDICE · 1813

MANSFIELD PARK · 1814

Emma · 1815

SANDITON (UNFINISHED) · 1871

Northanger Abbey · 1817

Persuasion · 1817

Lady Susan · 1871

GLOSSARY

ARISTOCRAT
Someone from the ruling class, usually with wealth and a title.

BREECHES
Men's knee-length pants, popular in the Regency era.

CHAPERONE
Someone who looks after and supervises another person.

CORONATION
The ceremony of crowning a king or queen.

CURRICLE
A light, two-wheeled carriage pulled by two horses side by side.

ELOPE
To run away secretly to get married.

FEMINISM
The belief in equal rights for men and women.

GENTRY
People of a high social class, usually landowners, just below the nobility.

GOTHIC FICTION
A style of writing that creates an atmosphere of fear and mystery.

GRAND TOUR
A cultural tour of Europe taken by young upper class men.

GRETNA GREEN
A village near the border in Scotland where couples could get married very quickly.

HEIR
A person who inherits the property of someone else when they die.

IRONY
When you write or say something but actually mean the opposite.

JANEITE
A fan of Jane Austen's work.

JUVENILIA
Works created by an author when they were young.

MILITIA
A group of citizens who train for military service to help the regular army in an emergency.

MINUET
A slow, graceful ballroom dance for two people.

PATRIARCHY
A society in which men hold the power.

PREJUDICE
An opinion formed about someone or something without any actual experience.

PSEUDONYM
A made-up name, especially one used by an author.

RECTORY
The house that a church organization provides for a priest to live in.

REGENCY
A period of time at the beginning of the 19th century when the Prince Regent ruled for the King in Britain.

SOCIAL CLASS
Grouping people together according to their wealth, job, and culture.

Button Books

First published 2021 by Button Books, an imprint of Guild of Master Craftsman Publications Ltd, Castle Place, 166 High Street, Lewes, East Sussex, BN7 1XU, UK. Copyright in the Work © GMC Publications Ltd, 2020. ISBN 978 1 78708 111 6. Distributed by Publishers Group West in the United States. All rights reserved. No part of this publication may be reproduced, stored in a retrieval system, or transmitted in any form or by any means without the prior permission of the publisher and copyright owner. While every effort has been made to obtain permission from the copyright holders for all material used in this book, the publishers will be pleased to hear from anyone who has not been appropriately acknowledged and to make the correction in future reprints. The publishers and authors can accept no legal responsibility for any consequences arising from the application of information, advice, or instructions given in this publication. A catalogue record for this book is available from the British Library. Senior Project Editor: Susie Duff. Design: Tim Lambert, Matt Carr, Jo Chapman. Illustrations: Alex Bailey, Matt Carr, Shutterstock. Color origination by GMC Reprographics. Printed and bound in China.